The Ten Commandments

© 2001 Christian Focus Publications
Geanies House, Fearn, Ross-shire, IV20 1TW
www.christianfocus.com

Text by Lois Veals
Illustrations by Jane Taylor
Cover design by Catherine Mackenzie
Printed by Bell and Bain, Glasgow
ISBN 1-85792-651-X

On some of the pages throughout this book you will be able to spot a dog and a cat. Look out for their expressions. They are happy when the children are being good and obedient but worried and concerned when the children are being disobdient. How many other animals can you spot in the pictures?

The Ten Commandments

by

Lois Veals

Contents

Introduction   7

1   The First Commandment
     Thou shalt have no other gods before Me   9

2   The Second Commandment
     Thou shalt not make unto thee any graven image   12

3   The Third Commandment
     Thou shalt not take the name of God in vain   14

4   The Fourth Commandment
     Remember the Sabbath Day to keep it holy   18

5   The Fifth Commandment
     Honour thy father and thy mother   21

6   The Sixth Commandment
     Thou shalt not kill   24

7   The Seventh Commandment
     Thou shalt not commit adultery   27

8   The Eighth Commandment
     Thou shalt not steal   30

9   The Ninth Commandment
     Thou shalt not bear false witness   33

10   The Tenth Commandment
     Thou shalt not covet   36

The Introduction

All important announcements have an "introduction". We need to know who is making the announcement and why or we will not take any notice. The Ten Commandments start with an introduction:

> I am the Lord thy God...

In the language in which the Bible was written, the word for Lord is JEHOVAH which was the most important name for God. It was used to remind people that God needs nothing but Himself. He is eternal and cannot change. He is so great that everyone must take notice of Him.

He is also our God because of the Lord Jesus Christ, who brings us together so that we are God's people, and He becomes our God. As He is our God, then He is our Father and friend who loves us and gives us all that we have. We can talk to Him, and He will talk to us through His Word. We always have Him as a friend.

> Which have brought thee out of the land of Egypt, out of the house of bondage.

Egypt was a terrible place for the children of Israel. The Egyptians worshipped strange gods - animals, birds, statues and even their king.

Many people today worship strange gods. We may know people who have a religion which is quite different from the Christian religion. Many people say, "It doesn't matter what god you believe in. It is all the same in the end."

The Bible teaches quite the opposite. We must worship the one true God, and we can only understand what He is like by studying the Bible. Some people say they worship God but it is not the God of the Bible.

The children of Israel were in "bondage". That means they were slaves, but the Lord brought them out of their misery. If we belong to Him, the Lord Jesus has saved us from the sin that made us slaves and now we are free. When we get to Heaven we shall be free of sin altogether.

When God first gave Moses the commandments, He called him up on to Mount Sinai. Moses was in the mountain for forty days and nights which reminds us of the Lord Jesus who was in the wilderness for forty days and nights. God gave Moses two pieces of stone with the commandments written on them with His own hand. Perhaps you can remember other times when God or the Lord Jesus wrote with His own hand. Do they have anything to do with the commandments?

When Moses came down from the mountain he heard a loud noise. It was the noise of feasting and dancing. The people had taken their golden earrings, melted them and made them into a calf to worship and sacrifice to. As Moses came nearer to the camp he saw the calf and the dancing, and he was very angry, and threw the stones out of his hands and broke them. Even before the people had received them, the commandments were broken!

This story is in Exodus chapter 32.

He is our God; and we are the people of his pasture (Psalm 95:7).

The First Commandment

> Thou shalt have no other gods before me.

As we try to understand what each of the commandments is teaching us, we shall say, "What does this tell me I must do?" and "What does this tell me I must not do?"

Nearly all the commandments begin with the word "thou" which means "you." If you have a modern translation of the Bible it probably says "you". The difference is that the commandments are for each person particularly. If your teacher says, "You are to stay in," she probably means the whole class. If she says "You, John, are to stay in," it means just John. The commandments are specially for you.

The first commandment tells us we are to worship only God. We can't do that unless we know all about Him so we must find out as much as we can. The Lord Jesus has shown us what God is like.

Here are some of the things we do if He is our God - remember Him, think about Him, love Him, believe Him, trust Him, be pleased with Him, work for Him, talk to Him, thank Him, praise Him, do what He wants and be sorry when we have not pleased Him.

We must not believe in another god, or say there is not God - that is easy to understand, but we can have other gods without realizing it. Some people trust in money. They think if only they were rich everything would be wonderful. Some people trust other people. If only so-and-so were in charge, everything would be all right. Others think that if everyone was clever and educated the world would be perfect. Even others think that if they do certain things, God will be pleased with them.

We must trust only God Himself. If we love something more than God, then we are not putting Him first. We can easily love other people, or things, or enjoy ourselves more than we love Him.

It says "before Me", to remind us that we can do nothing that God does not see. He expects everyone to put Him first and no-one will get away with disobeying Him.

Paul was in Athens in Greece. All the people there were eager to hear or to tell something new. Then Paul stood on Mars Hill and said,

"You men of Athens, I see you are too superstitious. As I watched you worship, I found an altar which said, 'TO THE UNKNOWN GOD'. I will tell you who it is you worship.

God, the Lord of Heaven and Earth, who made the world, does not live in temples made with hands. Nor can He be worshipped as man wants. He needs nothing - He gives life and breath and everything.

As we are made by God, we ought not to think He is like gold or silver or stone, made by man.

He tells everyone everywhere to repent, because He has chosen a day when He will judge the world through the Lord Jesus. He has proved this by raising Him from the dead."

When they heard this, some laughed at him, some said they would listen again, and some believed.

Read Acts chapter 17 for this story.

Know thou the God of thy father, and serve him with a perfect heart and with a willing mind (1 Chronicles 28:9).

These children have been playing all day long.
They might read their Bible later - if they have the time.
Are they keeping the first commandment?

The Second Commandment

> *Thou shalt not make unto thee any graven image...*
> *Thou shalt not bow down thyself to them...*

Before you read this chapter find Exodus chapter 20 in your Bible, and carefully read verses 4, 5 and 6 three times.

This commandment tells us how we must worship God. We must not make any statue or picture of God or of anything else to use for any kind of religious services.

We must remember that God is not like us. He is not to be worshipped by anything we do, such as bowing down to, or giving sacrifices to, anything made by men. We may say it is not our God, but just reminds us of Him. But it is still not right. It is quite wrong to bow our heads to altars or crosses or statues. This has become the custom in some churches because people have forgotten what God has said.

How are we to worship God? By praying, thanking Him in the name of Christ, reading the Bible and listening to the preaching and teaching of it. Our attitude is very important. King David said in Psalm 51:17: "The sacrifices of God are a broken spirit. A broken and a contrite (sorry) heart, O God, thou wilt not despise (turn away from)".

We are also told why we must obey this commandment.

God is a jealous God. We think of jealousy as wanting something for ourselves *which we should not have*. God wants everything for Himself because He has a right to it. That is why He is God. He will punish those who disobey Him (and often countries as well as particular people). If they are not punished in this life, people who disobey will be punished after death.

He will reward those who do what He wants. He forgives their sins and gives them great blessings both in this life and the next.

There was once a King called Manasseh. He did evil things in the sight of the Lord. He built altars to strange gods and worshipped and served them. He used witchcraft and wizards, and made God angry.

He set a carved image, an idol, in God's house and made the people sin even worse than the heathens. The Lord spoke to Manasseh and the people but they would not listen.

So the Lord sent the King of Assyria and his army, and they took Manasseh, and tied him in chains and took him away to Babylon.

There he was sorry, and prayed to God. God heard him and brought him back to Jerusalem. Manasseh realized that the Lord was God. He took away the strange gods and the idol from God's temple, and restored the true form of worship. He offered peace offerings and thank offerings to God, and told all the people to serve the Lord God of Israel.

This story is in 2 Chronicles chapter 33.

Worship the Lord in the beauty of holiness
(1 Chronicles 16:29).

These children are keeping the second
commandment by praising God as they sing.
What other ways are there of worshipping God?

The Third Commandment

Thou shalt not take the name of the Lord thy God in vain; for the Lord will not hold him guiltless that taketh his name in vain.

Names are very important. Your name is special to you. If two people with the same name live in the same house or are close friends, they are sometimes given nicknames. The nickname belongs to just one person.

God's name, and He has many (each one to show us something about Him), is special and belongs only to Him.

What does it mean to take His name in vain? What we call swearing is taking God's name in vain. We hear it all the time, on television, at school and even from people we know. We must be careful about what we say ourselves.

Another way is pretending to be something we are not. Some people seem so good when they are with Christian people but when they are with other friends you would not know they were supposed to be Christians.

Sometimes we promise God something and don't keep our promise. This is treating God's name lightly.

We can use God's name lightly by using it with good intentions but without thought of how great and holy He is. If you say, "Thank God', be careful that you really mean it.

We can even sing songs or wear badges which say something about the Lord Jesus but if we are not thinking of what we are saying or wearing, we are taking His name in vain.

This commandment, like the last, has a very stern warning. "The Lord will not hold him guiltless." Other people may not think it matters. There was a time in Britain when you could be punished for swearing but no-one takes any notice nowadays. People think that if they don't hurt anybody or anybody's property it doesn't really matter what they do. But God says to use His name lightly hurts Him which is even worse than hurting someone else.

Once, when Paul was in Ephesus, God worked special miracles by his hands. Handkerchiefs or aprons were taken from him to the sick people and their illnesses went away and evil spirits left them.

There were also some Jews in Ephesus who were the seven sons of a chief priest called Sceva. They tried to cure people who had evil spirits. Because they had heard what Paul was doing, they began to use the name of the Lord Jesus, and to say, "We command you by Jesus whom Paul preaches."

The evil spirit said, "Jesus I know and Paul I know, but who are you?" And the man who had the evil spirit jumped on them. He was stronger than they were, so they ran out of the house with their clothes torn off, and badly hurt.

This was heard by all the Jews and Greeks living at Ephesus, who became afraid. The name of the Lord Jesus was respected.

You will find this story in Acts chapter 19.

This people draweth nigh unto me with their mouth, and honoureth me with their lips, but their heart is far from me (Matthew 15 : 8).

People came to Paul with handkerchiefs belonging
to their sick friends and their friends were healed in the
name of the Lord Jesus. Why is Jesus' name so special?

The Fourth Commandment

Remember the Sabbath Day to keep it holy ...

Sabbath means rest. We are to remember the rest day. In Old Testament times it was to be the seventh day (or Saturday) but we now keep the first day, "The Lord's Day" (or Sunday).

Here are six questions and answers about the Sabbath.

1 *Why does God say, "remember"?*
   Because we must think of the day before it comes. We must try to do as much work as possible on Saturday. We must finish all our homework and make sure we are ready for school on Monday morning by Saturday night, so that Sunday can be kept special. Also we could easily forget about the one day in seven so He says remember.

2 *Why is this Commandment important?*
   Because all ten commandments are for all people at all times, whether they are Christians or not. Every Christian would say the other nine are important, so why should this one be different?

3 *How are we to keep it?*
   We must rest from the usual business of life. Of course there are some things which have to be done, but lots of jobs and games can be left for another day (especially if we have remembered the day before). We must do what we ought to do - go to church or Sunday School to worship God, read useful books and our Bibles, and help other people. If you help your mother on this day, she too will have more time to rest.

4 *Who is to keep it?*
   Everyone really should keep the Lord's Day. Our parents

are told to make sure that everyone in the house does no unnecessary work. Unfortunately very few people keep the Lord's day, and those of us who try are counted as strange and not enjoying life.

5 Why must we keep it?

Because God has asked for one day out of seven and it is right to give God what He asks. God remembered the day Himself after He had created the world. He rested on the seventh day and made it a holy day. Also it is good for us. We need one day in seven to rest from our work and refresh ourselves for the next week.

6 Why do we keep Sunday, not Saturday?

Jesus is Lord of the Sabbath. He made the day. In the New Testament the first day of the week is called, "The Lord's Day", and we know that is the day the apostles kept for worship. The reason for changing it was to show the great difference between the Creation and Redemption (Christ saving us from our sins). The old Sabbath was to remember the wonderful work of God in creating the world. The new Sabbath reminds us that Jesus' death and resurrection are the beginning of an even more wonderful work.

Nehemiah was a great man who rebuilt Jerusalem after it had been destroyed. What did he do to ensure the Sabbath was kept? He stopped people selling various items on the Sabbath by ordering the gates of the city to be shut during the Sabbath. Some of his servants stood guard at the gates to make sure that nobody broke the Sabbath.

Look in Nehemiah chapter 13 for this story.

The Son of Man is Lord of the Sabbath (Mark 2:28).

Nehemiah made sure that everyone in
Jerusalem kept the Sabbath day.
How can you keep Sunday holy?

The Fifth Commandment

> Honour thy father and thy mother
> that thy days may be long in the land
> which the Lord thy God giveth thee.

If we want to find out what a verse means, we have to look not just at the verse, but how the words are used in other places in the Bible. Here are some of the meanings of 'Father' and 'Mother'.

Father - Our own father. Someone who looks after us. Someone who looks after the poor. The King. An old man. God Himself.

Mother - Our own mother. Someone who looks after us. A lady more important than we are. Someone very dear to the Lord Jesus. The True Church of God.

We are told we must honour our father and our mother. They are placed over us by God, in His place. By honouring them we are honouring Him, and by having no respect for them we are having no respect for Him. We honour our father and mother by always speaking respectfully and not being rude. It is easy to be rude by what you do or how you look as well as by what you say. Another way to honour our parents is to always obey them, both by listening to what they have to teach, and by obeying their commands. You also honour them by helping and caring for them.

We cannot honour our parents without showing honour to our Heavenly Father. So we must obey Him as well.

This commandment says, "That thy days may be long in the land which the Lord thy God giveth thee." Disobedience to parents often shortens life, because their wisdom and awareness of danger helps them make rules for their children's safety. Long life is a special gift from God, but the person who honours his parents will have a happy life, however long it is.

There is a very sad story about a man who did not honour his father. King David had a son named Absalom whom he loved greatly. Absalom was very good-looking with thick long hair. But he had no respect for his father. When anyone came to King David with a problem, Absalom stood in the way, and told them that no-one from the King would hear them. If anyone bowed down to him he would shake his hand and kiss him. In this way, Absalom stole the hearts of the men of Israel.

After a while, when many people were on his side, Absalom plotted to overthrow his father so that he could be King instead. The day of the battle came. Before they went to fight David said to his captains, "Be gentle with Absalom." All the people heard what he said. The battle took place in a wood. David's men killed twenty thousand men of the other side.

Absalom met the servants of David. He was on a mule and it went under the boughs of a great oak tree. His head was caught in the tree and he was left hanging there while the mule went away. One of David's captains called Joab took three darts and killed Absalom.

When the news came to David he went to his room and cried. He said, "Oh my son Absalom, my son, my son Absalom! I wish God had let me die for you, Oh Absalom my son, my son!"

You can find this story in 2 Samuel 16,17 and 18.

> *And he (Jesus) went down with them, and came to Nazareth, and was subject unto them (Luke 2:51).*

This boy is honouring his parents by being helpful.
Can you think of things you can do to
honour your mother and father?

The Sixth Commandment

Thou shalt not kill

This seems to be easy to understand. The commandment tells us that we must not harm anyone - in fact we must do the opposite and try to help them in every way we can. We must not say anything unkind about them; we must never do anything that would hurt them; we must never set a bad example they might copy or encourage them to do wrong.

It also means we have to take care of ourselves. It is important that we should keep ourselves clean, eat good food and take exercise so that we look after our bodies. We should be careful not to take risks that would harm us. Be careful where you play, or how you cross the road. We must always watch out for others being hurt and warn them if they are in danger.

Many people do jobs which help save life. Sometimes they are paid, and sometimes they do it for nothing. There are doctors, nurses, policemen, firemen, lifeboat men, mountain rescue teams and lots of others. It is good that Christian people should do what they can in this way.

There are reasons for situations when we are allowed to kill. The Bible permits us to kill animals for food and clothes. However, we are also to care for them. Noah saved all the different kinds of animals in the Ark. If God knows of every sparrow that falls, then we must care too!

There have been times when countries have had to go to war to keep themselves free. Then it is necessary to kill in self-defence.

The Bible also teaches that it is sometimes necessary to

take people's lives as a punishment and as a warning to others, if they have done something very wrong. In some countries this still happens but in others they are put in prison instead.

Most of us would never think that we ourselves are murderers but the Bible tells us that 'whosoever hateth his brother is a murderer.' Brother here doesn't just mean a brother in your own family but any human being and particularly those who are your brothers and sisters through faith in the Lord Jesus Christ. Should we find that we have hateful thoughts in our hearts then we must go to Jesus and ask for His forgiveness.

On a mountain in Galilee our Lord Jesus, the greatest preacher of all, preached a sermon which we know as *The Sermon on the Mount.* In the sermon He explained very clearly God's Law which was first given in these Ten Commandments. He said that 'whosoever is angry with his brother without a cause shall be in danger of the judgment.' He reminds us that the wrong kind of anger is really heart-murder for the person who is angry in this way would kill if he could.

There are times when it is right and proper to be angry. God Himself is angry with the wicked every day (Psalm 7:11). We are to be angry against sin, while yet loving the sinner.

We must be very careful then that we are not committing murder in our hearts, either by hating other people or by being angry without a good cause.

To find out more of what Jesus said in His sermon read Matthew chapters 5-7.

> *Whosoever hateth his brother is a murderer: and ye know that no murderer hath eternal life abiding in him*
> (1 John 3:15)

God cared for the animals so he commanded
Noah to save them in the Ark. God cares for you too.
Can you think of ways that you can care
for people like God wants you to do?

The Seventh Commandment

Thou shalt not commit adultery

Before we look closely at this seventh commandment, find Genesis chapter 2 and then read verses 21-24, very carefully. God made Adam and then gave him a wife. Adam and Eve loved each other and lived happily together and God saw that it was 'very good'. God planned it to be that way and that is the way He still wants it to be. There was one husband, Adam, and one wife, Eve - just one of each - and together they had a family.

God commanded it to be that way right through Bible times and up to the present day. When a man and a woman get married they make certain promises before God, to stay together forever and to be with each other through every situation that will come their way. Yet some men and women do not keep these promises. Instead they choose to break God's law and this seventh commandment.

Instead of the "one man" and the "one woman" staying with each other for ever, sadly, something very different sometimes happens in our world today. A man might leave his wife and live with another woman. Or a woman might leave her husband just because she has found another man whom she wants to be with instead. They are breaking God's commandment by doing these things. It brings so much hurt and pain to a family when a father or mother decides to leave the home and children suffer a lot as a result. Breaking God's law always brings unhappiness and pain.

In Bible times a man or woman would be killed for breaking this seventh commandment. This helps us to see just how important it is in God's eyes. It is really a command for us to obey when we are grown up , but it is good for us to know about it and understand it while we are growing up. This seventh commandment is just as important as all the other commandments.

We have all heard of David, the shepherd boy who became a king. He was a great man of God, yet he broke this very commandment! One evening, while King David was walking on the flat roof of his house, he saw a very beautiful woman washing herself. David wanted that woman for himself, even when the messengers told him that she was somebody else's wife! He had her brought to his house and sinned before God by breaking this seventh commandment. What David did was very wrong and God punished him for that disobedience.

The whole story can be found in the second book of Samuel, chapters 11 and 12. David loved God but he still sinned before Him and broke His law.

It is the same today. When we ask God to come into our hearts and lives we must still try just as hard to keep His commandments. In many ways it becomes more difficult because the Devil is always there, trying his best to make us go the wrong way, do the wrong thing and forget about God. We must ask God, daily, to help us obey Him in everything we do.

> *Husbands, love your wives, even as Christ also loved the church, and gave himself for it* (Ephesians 5:25).

When a couple marry they make promises to each other
but also to God. What do they promise to do?

The Eighth Commandment

Thou shalt not steal

This commandment may seem straightforward enough to us as we read it - "do not steal". We all know what that means. We should not go out and take something that does not belong to us. It is wrong to steal money or anything else from other people. It is also wrong to take things from shops without paying. God's law makes it clear that to steal is very wrong and we should always remember that God sees everything we do.

Stealing can mean a few other things too. Let's look at three examples.

1. Perhaps we are sitting an exam or test and we copy some answers from someone sitting beside us. We are stealing that person's knowledge and we are stealing extra, undeserved marks for ourselves.

2. Imagine it is Sports Day. We are all running a race together. We can see the finishing post but someone is just in front of us. Maybe we trip that person up and make it look like an accident. We run on to get the first place and prize. Yet we have stolen both these things from the real winner.

3. Perhaps again we have been paid money to do a special job thoroughly. Instead of taking the time to do it properly we quickly rush through the job, doing as little as possible, as quickly as we can. We then rush off to spend our not very well earned cash.

In their way these three examples all show how we can break the eighth commandment - "do not steal". There are many other examples in our lives if we look for them.

There are also many examples of stealing to be found in God's Word. If you turn to Joshua chapter 7, you will read about a man called Achan. He broke this commandment and was put to death because of his disobedience.

When the Children of Israel captured the city of Jericho, God commanded that the Israelites should not keep anything in it for themselves - no slaves, no animals, no treasures - nothing. Yet this man Achan sinned before God by stealing. He decided to steal some lovely clothes, some gold and some silver. He hid all these things in his tent. God was angry because of Achan's sin. He was not with the Israelites as He had been in previous times. They had to flee before the men of Ai.

God then spoke to Joshua and told him that someone amongst the Israelites had sinned by stealing and disobeying God's command. The very next morning Joshua gathered together all the people, tribe by tribe, family by family, household by household, until finally Achan stood before him. Achan was wrong to steal and break God's law and he was put to death. Perhaps he thought no-one had seen him stealing, and so he would never be found out.

God sees us. He sees us all the time - every moment of our lives. We should always remember that. Each new day we should ask God, who loves us dearly, to help us obey Him in the way we live our lives.

> *Let him that stole, steal no more: but rather let him labour, working with his hands the thing which is good, that he may have to give to him that needeth* (Ephesians 4 : 28).

This boy thinks that there are so many sweets in his friend's pocket that he won't notice if some are missing. Does that mean it's all right to take some without asking?

The Ninth Commandment

Thou shalt not bear false witness ...

This ninth commandment tells us that we must never tell lies. We might think that a lie is just a little thing and not very important compared to other sins such as killing or stealing. Yet we find that it is here as one of God's Ten Commandments. There are many times when we tell lies. Every time we lie we are doing wrong.

What is a lie?

We lie when we decide not to tell "the truth, the whole truth, and nothing but the truth". Witnesses in a courtroom promise to tell the truth about what they know. They realise just how important that promise or oath is as they speak and give evidence. It should be our promise too as we are growing up. God's law demands complete honesty from us at all times and in every situation.

Why do we tell lies? Sometimes we do something wrong but rather than own up to it at once, we tell a lie. We say we didn't do it or, worse still, we put the blame on someone else. It takes courage to own up to wrong-doing. We need to be truthful, even if that can be very difficult.

Sometimes we tell lies to excuse our behaviour. If we are late for school we could say that we "slept in" when, in honesty, we should say that we dawdled along the road. If we have chores or homework we could say that we hadn't time to do them. That would be another lie if, in honesty, we should say that we were playing or watching television. These are lies - not "tiny lies", "excuses" or "good reasons", but lies. We should remember that.

Ananias and Sapphira were two people in the Bible who told a lie and we can find their story in Acts chapter 5. If we read chapter 4, verses 34 and 35, that sets the scene for us.

When Ananias and Sapphira sold their land they brought their money to Peter. No-one made them do that. It was their own choice. They could have kept it all for themselves. Or they could have given some of it and kept the rest - as long as they were honest about it. They made the wrong choice. It made them look very good to be seen giving all their money. Yet they planned together to tell a lie about the money they were giving. They said it was all the money but they had actually kept some of it for themselves without saying anything about it. They lied to Peter. His answer was, "Thou hast not lied unto men but unto God." Both Ananias and Sapphira could have told the truth - all the truth - about the money, but they chose to lie and disobey God's law by breaking this commandment.

Lying is something we do on purpose, not something we cannot help. Ananias and Sapphira listened to the Devil, who likes to see us doing the wrong thing by breaking God's commandments. We should pray for strength from God to resist the Devil when he tempts us to lie and do wrong.

When he (the Devil) speaketh a lie, he speaketh of his own, for he is a liar, and the father of it (John 8:44).

This girl's brother is always getting into trouble so she knows her dad will believe her when she says that it was his fault; even if it wasn't.
It doesn't really matter anyway .... or does it?

The Tenth Commandment

> *Thou shalt not covet ....*

To "covet" means to want very much something that we cannot have, or something that belongs to someone else. This commandment forbids us to want things that we see our neighbour has such as his house, his family or his possessions. It ends by saying that we are not to covet ANYTHING that is our neighbour's.

To begin with, we must realise that our neighbours are not just the people who live next door to us. Our "neighbour" refers to everyone we meet. So we must not want the things we see other people have. We must learn to be happy with what we ourselves have been given. It is much better to look at God's goodness in giving us all that we have, than to spend miserable lives being jealous of what others around us possess.

Being contented makes our lives peaceful and fulfilled and the material things of the world around us become very unimportant to us. (These things are not lasting anyway and will soon pass away.) This commandment is very much echoed in the New Testament, where we are continually reminded to keep God's law.

We must also look at this commandment in another way. God wants us also to be careful not to envy our neighbours themselves! Perhaps we have a popular, lively, talented friend, whereas we are shy, quiet and reserved. Yet we must not covet our friend's abilities.

Instead we should look at ourselves and discover our own God-given strengths and abilities. We should thank God for these as we seek to develop our own individuality.

Each one of us is unique and is special to God. He is to be praised for creating us just as we are.

We read in Acts chapter 8 verses 9-24 about a man called Simon the Sorcerer. He coveted the power of the Apostles. He wanted it so badly, in fact, that he offered to pay money for that power which he did not have. Simon saw that, when the Apostles laid their hands on people, the Holy Spirit was given to them.

His heart was not right in God's sight and he just wanted to have power over people. He was envious of the Apostles and wanted to be able to do what they were doing. He tried to bribe them. This shows us how envy and jealousy can lead us into lots of other sins.

Hebrews chapter 13 verse 5 is a wonderful verse to learn and remember every day: "Let your conversation be without covetousness, and be content with such things as ye have, for he hath said, I will never leave you nor forsake thee." What does it matter what we do or do not have in this world if Jesus Christ is our Lord and Saviour. We have and we are everything - in Him.

> *Take heed, and beware of covetousness: for a man's life consisteth not in the abundance of the things which he possesseth* (Luke 12: 15).

Maybe you think your friends have more and better things than you do and you hear yourself saying 'it's not fair!' What should you do when you feel like this?

God says ....

Have no other gods before me.

Do not make any graven images.

Do not take the Lord's name in vain.

Keep the Sabbath day holy.

Honour your father and mother.

Do not kill.

Do not commit adultery.

Do not steal.

Do not bear false witness.

Do not covet.

CHRISTIAN FOCUS

Good books with the real message of hope!

Christian Focus Publications publishes biblically-accurate books for adults and children.

If you are looking for quality Bible teaching for children then we have a wide and excellent range of Bible story books - from board books to teenage fiction, we have it covered.

You can also try our new Bible teaching Syllabus for 3-9 year olds and teaching materials for pre-school children.

These children's books are bright, fun and full of biblical truth, an ideal way to help children discover Jesus Christ for themselves. Our aim is to help children find out about God and get them enthusiastic about reading the Bible, now and later in their lives.

Find us at our web page:
www.christianfocus.com